COLUMBUS
AND THE
AGE OF EXPLORERS

By Nadia Higgins

Content Advisor:
Brian W. Ogilvie
Associate Professor of History
University of Massachusetts, Amherst

Rourke
Publishing LLC
Vero Beach, Florida 32964

EVENTS IN AMERICAN HISTORY

www.rourkepublishing.com

Image Credits:
Library of Congress, cover (top left and right), 1, 4, 7, 8, 9, 10, 12, 13, 14 (top), 15, 18, 19, 20, 22, 23, 24, 25, 27, 30, 31, 32, 35, 37, 38, 40, 41, 42, 43, 44, 45, 46; iStockphoto, cover (bottom left), 5, 14, 16, 17, 21, 28-29, 36, 39; PhotoDisk© 11, Phil Martin Photography, 34

Editorial Direction: Red Line Editorial, Inc.; Bob Temple

Editor: Nadia Higgins

Designer: Lindaanne Donohoe

Fact Research: Laurie Kahn

Library of Congress Cataloging-in-Publication Data

Higgins, Nadia.
  Columbus and the age of explorers / by Nadia Higgins.
    p. cm. — (Events in American history)
  Includes bibliographical references and index.
  ISBN 1–60044–119–X (hardcover)
  ISBN 978-1-60044-353-4 (paperback)
  1. Columbus, Christopher—Juvenile literature. 2. America—Discovery and
exploration—Spanish—Juvenile literature. 3. America—Discovery and
exploration—European—Juvenile literature. 4.
Explorers—Spain—Biography—Juvenile literature. 5.
Explorers—Europe—Biography—Juvenile literature. 6.
Explorers—America—Biography—Juvenile literature. I. Title.
  E111.H6 2007
  970.01'5—dc22
                                      2006018735

Printed in the USA

Rourke

Publishing LLC
Vero Beach, Florida 32964

Table of Contents

Chapter One

Columbus Arrives in the Americas

The crew aboard the *Niña*, the *Pinta*, and the *Santa María* was getting restless. The 90 men had been at sea for more than two months already. Where were they? Would their food supplies hold up long enough? Would they be able to find their way back to Spain?

Their captain, Christopher Columbus, knew that he was about to have a mutiny on his hands. But Columbus was not ready to turn around. He had promised King Ferdinand and Queen Isabella of Spain that this voyage would be a success. Perhaps more important, he had spent most of his adult life planning this trip. Columbus swore that he could sail west from Spain halfway around the world. He was determined to be the first to find a water route to what was called the Indies, the eastern part of Asia.

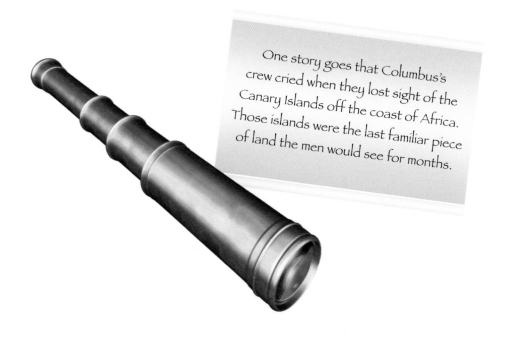

One story goes that Columbus's crew cried when they lost sight of the Canary Islands off the coast of Africa. Those islands were the last familiar piece of land the men would see for months.

Columbus anxiously scanned the seas for any sign of land. Then, on October 7, 1492, birds were sighted. Land had to be close by. Columbus declared that the first sailor to spot land would receive a handsome reward.

Sure enough, at 2 a.m. on October 12, 1492, a Spanish sailor aboard the *Pinta* woke up the men shouting, *"Tierra! Tierra!"* Land! Land! Dimly lit by moonlight, the shore lay above the black water.

Later that morning, Columbus became the first European to step on the white sand of that land. Almost immediately, natives arrived at the beach with great curiosity. The islanders were unlike anybody the Spaniards had ever seen. Most of them were naked. Their bodies were decorated with black, red, and white paint.

"I therefore gave red caps to some and glass beads to others. They hung the beads around their necks, along with some other things of slight value that I gave them. And they took great pleasure in this and became so friendly that it was a marvel. They traded and gave everything they had with good will, but it seems to me that they have very little and are poor in everything. I warned my men to take nothing from the people without giving them something in exchange."

The Log of Christopher Columbus

"Today I made 180 miles at a speed of 7½ knots. I recorded only 144 miles in order not to alarm the sailors if the voyage is lengthy."

The Log of Christopher Columbus

Columbus believed he had successfully discovered a water route to Asia. The natives, he thought, were from an island in the East Indies, near Japan or China. He called them *Indians*—the word we still use today. But Columbus was still thousands of miles from Asia. What he didn't know—what no European knew—was that North and South America blocked the way from Europe to Asia. In reality, Columbus was on the shore of an island in the Bahamas, south of what is now Florida.

Columbus sailed across the Atlantic in a small, wooden ship with sails.

The Taino People

No one knows for sure which island Columbus landed on. The natives called it Guanahani. These islanders were probably Taino.

Columbus described the Taino people as being tall and tan. They had straight hair, which they knotted in the back. They had a custom of binding their heads, which made their foreheads wide and flat.

Columbus often referred to the Taino as a kind, gentle people. At the same time, he considered them "primitive"—in part because of their lack of clothing and guns. In reality, the Taino had a highly developed culture.

The Taino were skilled farmers. They made cotton cloth, pottery, and wood carvings. They built large, wooden canoes that could hold more than 100 people. The swift boats were used for fishing. The Taino also paddled to nearby islands, where they traded with neighboring communities.

The natives lived close to one another in thatch houses. They often gathered at a central plaza for meetings and dances. Boys and girls played games with rubber balls. Tobacco leaves were lit and passed around as an act of friendship. In fact, the word *tobacco* comes from the Taino, as do other words such as *hammock*, *hurricane*, and *canoe*.

An illustration from the late 1800s shows Columbus and members of his crew soon after landing in the Bahamas. The Spaniards brought small objects, such as beads and bells, to trade with the native people.

"I sent the ship's boat ashore for water, and those on the island, with very good will, showed my people where the water was. They even carried the full casks to the boat and took great delight in pleasing us."

The Log of Christopher Columbus

A map from the 1500s shows the coast of present-day Virginia.

Columbus died insisting that he had landed in Asia. He would have been sorely disappointed to learn otherwise. However, his voyage turned out to be much more important than he could ever imagine. From Europe's point of view, Columbus had discovered the New World. These new lands promised great wealth. Soon Spain, Portugal, Great Britain, and France began sending more explorers. They competed with one another to find land and claim it for their countries. European settlers arrived and set up colonies on the land.

During the few decades following Columbus's 1492 journey, explorers sailed around Africa. They sailed up and down the east coast of the Americas. They sailed around the globe. The map of the world was entirely redrawn. This period in history came to be known as the Age of Discovery.

Chapter Two

Before Columbus

In the early 1500s, much of North America was wild land. Thick forests covered areas that we know today as New England, New York, the Carolinas, and Florida. Wild bears roamed almost everywhere. Also common were cougars, skunks, opossums, and squirrels. Fish swarmed in rivers and lakes. Mosquitoes buzzed in huge clouds. Pigeons were so numerous, it was said they blocked out the sun for hours at a time.

"[The island] has trees of a thousand kinds, and all have their kinds of fruit, and all so fragrant that it is marvelous."

The Log of Christopher Columbus

Though much of the land was untouched, it was not empty. In fact, 40 million American Indians lived there. That is about the same number of people who lived in Western Europe at the time.

The ancestors of these Indians were the first humans to arrive in North America. They came from Asia as much as 50,000 years ago. They walked into Alaska over land or ice that no longer exists.

For many years, no new explorers arrived. Then, in 1000, Vikings from Norway reached North America by sailing west from Europe. They even tried to start a colony in what is now Newfoundland, an island off the coast of Canada. Life proved to be too harsh in this new land, however. The Vikings gave up and left for good.

An illustration from 1591 shows how one European artist pictured American Indian teenagers at play.

Explorers reported that they could smell the sweet trees and flowers of the New World as they approached land. The scent carried for miles out to sea.

Viking explorer Leif Ericson (ca. 980–ca. 1025) led what was likely the first European expedition to North America.

The Life of Christopher Columbus

Christopher Columbus was born sometime in the late summer or early fall of 1451 in Genoa, Italy. His Italian name was Cristoforo Colombo. For most of his life, however, he called himself Cristóbal Colón, the Spanish version of his name.

At 14, Columbus began sailing on trading ships. At 25, he was shipwrecked off the coast of Portugal. He settled in Lisbon, Portugal, where he met and married a Portuguese noblewoman. She and Columbus had one son before she died.

After Columbus's 1492 trip, he returned to the Americas three more times. As part of his agreement with Ferdinand and Isabella, Columbus had been granted governorship over all new colonies. One important colony was on the island of Hispaniola, now home to the Dominican Republic and Haiti. At one point, the settlers of the colony revolted. A new governor was sent to replace Columbus. When he refused to give up his post, Columbus was arrested and sent back to Spain in chains. The Spanish rulers dropped charges against Columbus on the condition that he never return to Hispaniola again.

Until his death at age 55, Columbus insisted that he'd reached the Indies. He died an unhappy and disappointed man.

Christopher Columbus as a young man

Columbus probably had no knowledge of the Viking explorers. Few in his time would have imagined that Europeans had sailed so far away before. A common story goes that people in the 1400s believed the world was flat. They feared sailing off its edge. In fact, most sailors knew the world was round but feared that strange and fantastic creatures lived far out in the seas. Some thought that if they traveled past a certain point, they'd be sucked under by a giant whirlpool.

Columbus refused to believe such stories. Born in the seaside town of Genoa, Italy, Columbus grew up surrounded by sailors. Columbus himself became a sailor at an early age.

An antique compass

This 1562 map of North and South America shows monsters lurking in the waters of the Atlantic Ocean.

Columbus probably did not learn to read or write until he was an adult. Once he learned, however, he read widely on the subjects of geography and navigation. His reading convinced him of two things. The first was that most of the world was covered by land. The other was that Asia was just 3,000 miles (4,800 kilometers) due west of Europe. Columbus was mistaken on both points. In reality, water covers most of the globe, and Asia is about 12,000 miles (19,000 kilometers) west of Europe. However, Columbus's miscalculations were important because they convinced him that he could find a direct water route to the Indies.

Developments in Ships and Sailing

During the Age of Discovery, great progress was made in the art of building and guiding ships. The introduction of a ship called a caravel meant that sailors could better control their routes. Old ocean-going ships had square sails, which meant they could only go forward when the winds were behind them. Caravels had both square and triangular sails, which allowed them to sail into a wind by following a zigzag course. The ships were also lighter than older ships. They could sail in the shallow water along a coastline.

Sea captains had the use of several instruments to measure a ship's position at sea. A type of compass called a wind rose was available. However, many, including Columbus, did not trust it. They relied on instruments called astrolabes and quadrants that used the stars and shadows to measure the position of the ship. These tools had a significant drawback, however: They could tell how far a ship had traveled north or south—but not east or west.

Finding a water route to the Indies was of utmost importance. By the fifteenth century, Europe had come to rely on trade with countries such as India, China, and Japan. For more than a hundred years, the Asian countries provided silk, jewels, and —most important to the Europeans— spices. In those days, meat was dried with salt to keep it from rotting. (And if the meat did rot, it was eaten anyway.) The spices covered the taste of bad or salted meat.

The problem was that the land route to the Indies was dangerous and expensive—and slow. The goods were carried hundreds of miles by camels. Many European rulers were eager to find a water route.

A quadrant was a tool that relied on the stars to help sailors find their way across the open sea.

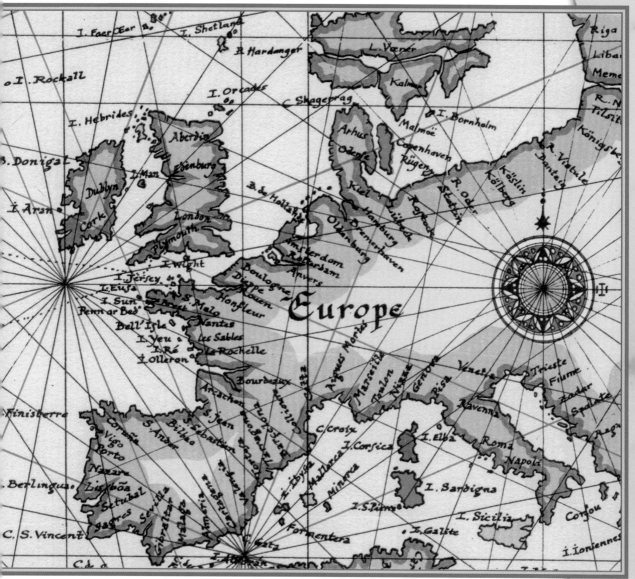

Europe during the fifteenth century

Portugal is a small seaside country located along the western edge of Spain. In the fifteenth century, it ruled the seas around Europe. Portuguese explorers had made great progress in finding an eastern route to the Indies. But the route was long—it went all the way around the southern tip of Africa.

Columbus thought a western route would be quicker because he believed there was no land in the way. In 1481, Columbus took his idea to King John II of Portugal, who turned him down. It was too far, too dangerous, and too expensive. During the next four years, Columbus continued to try to convince King John II, but was always turned down. Portugal was more interested in finding an eastern route to Asia by going around Africa.

Next Columbus took his plan to Spain. King Ferdinand and Queen Isabella arranged a group of scholars to study the plan. After four years, they too pronounced Columbus's ideas unsound. During this time, Columbus went to Great Britain and France, which also rejected his proposal.

One story goes that Columbus had so much trouble finding willing sailors to sign up for the 1492 voyage that one-fourth of his crew were prisoners. They joined only because they were promised their freedom upon returning to Spain.

"From a very young age, I began to follow the sea and have continued to do so to this day. This art of navigation incites those who pursue it to enquire into the secrets of the world."

1501 letter from Columbus to Ferdinand and Isabella

His request granted, Columbus kneels before Queen Isabella in gratitude.

Then in 1492, Spain won an important war. With extra money in hand, Ferdinand and Isabella reconsidered Columbus's plan. The risks were great—but if all went well, the outcome would be worth it. Little did any of them know that instead of finding Asia, Columbus would find North and South America.

Chapter Three

Mapping the Americas

In the late fifteenth century, world maps were works of art. Many were painted on soft animal skin. Mapmakers decorated their work with imaginary creatures and countries. The maps showed just three continents—Europe, Africa, and Asia. The Atlantic Ocean was called the Ocean Sea. North and South America were absent from the maps, as was the Pacific Ocean. The maps showed a globe much smaller than it actually was.

Little by little, the maps became more accurate after Columbus. Europe buzzed with excitement about the lands he described. More and more expeditions were planned. The explorers landed at different places along the coasts of North and South America. Each voyage added information to the previous one about the size and shape of the continents.

In the early 1500s, reliable clocks as we know them were not known. To measure time, each ship had a sandglass. It looked similar to the sand-filled timers used in some board games today. Each half-hour, the sandglass was turned, and a bell was rung.

John Cabot explored the shores of northern North America with his son, Sebastian.

John Cabot had a son, Sebastian, who was also an explorer. Historians think that Sebastian may have tried to take credit for his father's work. That is why so little is known about the details of Cabot's journeys.

In May 1497, John Cabot headed west from England. Like Columbus, he believed he would reach Asia. But Cabot's route was hundreds of miles north of the one Columbus had taken. Cabot believed this northern route would carry him more quickly to the riches of the Indies.

Not much is known about Cabot's journey. He left on a small ship, the *Matthew*, with a crew of 18 sailors. As they headed across the Atlantic, strong winds pushed against the ship's sails. As it turned out, Cabot's voyage took about the same amount of time as Columbus's, though only half the distance was covered.

On June 24, Cabot went ashore. Historians are not sure exactly where he landed. It was somewhere along the east coast of Canada or on the coast of Maine. Cabot claimed the cold, rocky land for Great Britain.

No natives came to greet Cabot. However, Cabot did see signs that people lived nearby. He found fishing nets and traps for catching wild animals. Cabot did not find the jewels and spices he was looking for. Instead, he found another kind of treasure: The waters along the coast were full of fish. The men had only to lower a basket into the ocean to catch them.

How the Americas Got Their Name

The Italian Amerigo Vespucci got credit for being the first to call the Americas a New World. Between 1499 and 1502, Vespucci sailed to South America two times. During those voyages, he studied the position of the moon and planets. This led him to believe that Earth was quite a bit larger than people had thought. Vespucci's estimates of the size of Earth were amazingly accurate. He concluded that the lush, green lands Columbus described were too close to Europe to be part of Asia.

Vespucci put his ideas in a letter that was published in Florence, Italy. He wrote: "These regions we may rightly call . . . a New World, because our ancestors had no knowledge of them. . . . I have found a continent more densely populated in animals than our Europe or Asia or Africa."

News of Amerigo Vespucci's ideas spread. In 1507, a German mapmaker used *America*, the Latin version of *Amerigo*, to label the continent. The name stuck.

Cabot returned to England thinking that he had reached Asia. King Henry VII received the explorer with a hero's welcome. Soon Cabot was sent west again—this time with five ships. The mission proved to be ill-fated. Only one ship made it back, and Cabot himself was lost at sea.

Though Cabot was never heard from again, his first voyage turned out to be even more important than he had thought. It showed geographers just how far north the Americas extended.

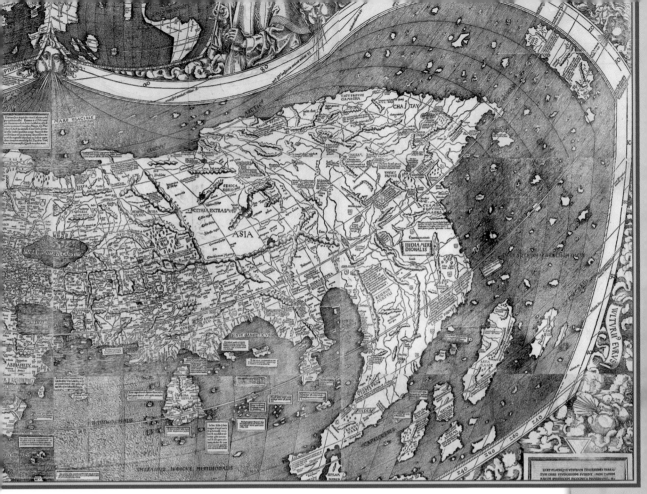

The first map to use "America" to label the New World

Cabot's arrival in North America also led to the founding of British colonies about a hundred years later.

It only took a few years for people to realize that Cabot and Columbus had landed not in the Indies but on a new continent. The Spanish explorer Vasco Núñez de Balboa provided more proof that the New World was not Asia. It was its own landmass located between two oceans. In 1501, Balboa traveled to the New World in search of fortune. For almost ten years, he lived in a Spanish settlement on an island off the eastern shore of Central America. Life was hard here. Balboa tried to get by as a pig farmer but fell heavily into debt.

Balboa hoped to have better luck on another colony on the mainland. To escape his creditors, he hid in a barrel aboard a ship that was carrying new settlers to the colony. When he arrived, however, he discovered that the new colony no longer existed. Lack of food and Indian attacks had driven the settlers away. Balboa led a group of survivors inland. They settled a new village, Darién, and made Balboa its governor.

Balboa led teams of explorers into the surrounding area. He battled with some Indians and befriended others. One group of Indians told Balboa about a land where gold was plentiful. The land, called Tubanama, was on the other side of mountains by an ocean.

In 1513, Balboa organized an expedition to Tubanama. With 190 Spaniards and several Indian guides, Balboa trudged through the jungles of what is now Panama. Following Indian trails, Balboa walked across the continent's narrowest point. As he approached the ocean, he told his men to stay behind. He continued to a mountaintop, where he became the first European to see the eastern shore of the Pacific Ocean. He claimed the ocean and all the lands beyond it for the king of Spain.

Balboa called the ocean he saw the South Sea, since it lay south of the strip of land from which he first viewed it. Magellan was the one who named the ocean *Pacific*, which means *peaceful*.

Standing on the coast of present-day Panama, Balboa claims the Pacific Ocean for Spain.

Six years later, Ferdinand Magellan set out across the Atlantic Ocean from Spain. The Portuguese explorer was sailing under the Spanish flag. Like Columbus, he was looking for a water route to Asia. However, Magellan now understood what Columbus had not: He would have to sail all the way around the southern tip of South America. Indeed, he would have to cross not just the Atlantic Ocean but the Pacific as well.

Ferdinand Magellan

Crossing the Pacific, Magellan's crew ran completely out of food. Many men died. The survivors resorted to eating sawdust and rats.

It took members of Magellan's crew three years to circle the globe. Today the trip can be done in less than a full day by jet.

The trip was much longer than Magellan had thought, and full of incredible hardship. When Magellan set sail, he had five ships and a crew of about 240. Three years later, just one boat and 18 survivors sailed back to Spain. The worm-eaten boats were so leaky they could barely stay afloat. The crew was half-starved. Their captain, Magellan, had died in battle the previous year. But Magellan's expedition had not only succeeded in finding a water route around South America. His crew had sailed around the world.

Chapter Four

In Search of Riches

While Magellan's crew was sailing across the Pacific, Spain was sending other missions to explore the lands of Central and South America. These adventurers were called conquistadors—the Spanish word for conquerors. Unlike earlier explorers, they had little interest in maps or navigation. They were soldiers who came in search of gold and power. Many came with priests in order to convert the Indians to Christianity.

Hernando de Soto arrives on the banks of the Mississippi. The Spanish conquistador led the first European expedition to the famous river in 1541.

"It was a miracle that these wonderful lands had remained unknown to the rest of the world through all history, and were saved by God to be discovered in our time."

Pedro Cieza de Leon, conquistador

Juan Ponce de Léon

Some conquistadors traveled into areas that are now part of the United States. Juan Ponce de León sailed to Florida. Hernando de Soto led more than 600 men through what became Georgia, Alabama, Mississippi, and Arkansas. In the west, Francisco Vásquez de Coronado led a 7,000-mile (11,200 kilometers) journey through present-day Arizona, New Mexico, Texas, Oklahoma, and Kansas.

Conquistadors such as Hernan Cortes and Francisco Pizarro had found incredible riches in Mexico and South America. However, those who explored parts of the modern-day United States did not discover the gold they sought. But their combined adventures gave Europeans a good idea of the breadth of North America.

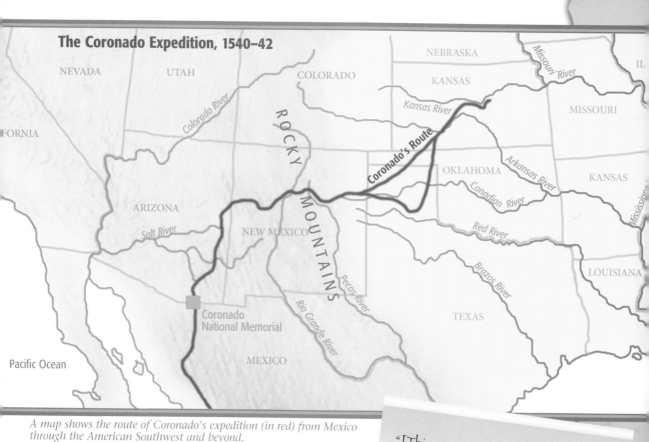

The Coronado Expedition, 1540–42

NEVADA · UTAH · COLORADO · NEBRASKA · KANSAS · IL · MISSOURI · KANSAS

Colorado River · Kansas River · Missouri River · Coronado's Route · OKLAHOMA · Arkansas River

ARIZONA · NEW MEXICO · Canadian River · MISSISSIPPI

Salt River · ROCKY MOUNTAINS · Red River · LOUISIANA

Coronado National Memorial · Pecos River · Rio Grande River · Brazos River · TEXAS

Pacific Ocean · MEXICO

A map shows the route of Coronado's expedition (in red) from Mexico through the American Southwest and beyond.

> "[This country has a] fine appearance, the like of which I have never seen anywhere in our Spain, Italy, or any part of France. ... It is not a hilly country, but has [plateaus], plains, and charming rivers with fine waters."
>
> Juan Jaramillo, one of Coronado's captains, describing the Great Plains of central Kansas

In 1538, Coronado was governor of a province of Mexico. At that time, rumors were flying about the Seven Cities of Cíbola, supposedly located to the north. These cities were said to have buildings made from bricks of pure gold. The legends were of great interest to the 28-year-old conquistador. He had been on a search for wealth for many years. Coronado had been born into a rich family in Spain. However, Coronado was left to find his own fortune after his older brother inherited all the family's wealth. So, three years earlier, he had left for the New World to start a new life.

EVENTS IN AMERICAN HISTORY

The Search for the Northwest Passage

While Spain was finding treasure in South America, France wondered how it too could find wealth in the New World. Competing with a powerful country like Spain was out of the question. So French explorers headed north.

Magellan had found a water route to Asia around the southern tip of South America. The king of France wondered if his country could find an even shorter water route across or around North America. In 1524, Giovanni da Verrazano, an Italian sailing under the French flag, began the search for what became known as the Northwest Passage. Verrazano did not find the passage, but he explored the eastern coast of North America from North Carolina to Newfoundland, Canada.

The search for the Northwest Passage continued for hundreds of years. The British and Dutch also sent expeditions. They often came back with important findings about islands, rivers, and bays along the Atlantic coast. They claimed land for their countries. But the first expedition to sail all the way through the Northwest Passage would be commanded by a Norwegian. In 1906, Roald Amundsen's ship, the *Gjoa*, sailed from the Atlantic to the Pacific through islands of northern Canada and around Alaska.

In February 1540, Coronado set out in search of the golden cities. With him were some 300 Spanish soldiers and 1,000 Indian servants and soldiers. Many of the Indian men traveled with their wives and children. The expedition set out from a small Mexican town with 1,000 horses. Live cattle, sheep, and pigs were brought along in case food became scarce along the way.

Instead of gold cities, Coronado found Indian pueblos, or villages, such as this one preserved at Mesa Verde National Park in Colorado.

This 1897 illustration shows Coronado leading his soldiers through the deserts of the American Southwest.

It was a difficult journey. The soldiers trekked through the deserts of present-day Arizona and New Mexico. After four months, they arrived at one of the Seven Cities of Cíbola. But instead of a gold city, they found a small village with stone and mud houses. About a hundred families of Zuni Indians lived here. Coronado was bitterly disappointed.

By now, the Spaniards were running extremely low on food. Coronado gave the order to attack the city. The Zunis fought to defend their village. They threw stones at the Europeans. They fired arrows through openings in the walls and from their roofs. Wearing a gold suit of armor, Coronado was an easy target in the bright sun. An arrow stabbed him in the foot. Nevertheless, the Spaniards defeated the Zunis and took the Indians' stores of food.

After this, Coronado's army split up to explore both east and west. One group traveled 20 days in search of water. They came upon one of the most beautiful sites in the natural world. Gazing into the Grand Canyon of Arizona, the conquistadors were disappointed. They could not reach the rushing waters of the Colorado River at the bottom of the giant hole.

"[I was told] there is much gold and that the natives . . . make it into vessels and ornaments for their ears."

Marcos de Niza, a Spanish priest dispatched by Coronado to find Cíbola and report back to the conquistador (this description proved false)

Coronado and his men eventually wandered as far as central Kansas. They became the first Europeans to see the Great Plains. They marveled at huge herds of buffalo that traveled over the flat land.

The Spaniards walked over land rich in gold and silver, but the precious metals would not be discovered for many years. In 1542, Coronado headed back to Mexico on a stretcher pulled by mules. Many of Coronado's men left his army rather than go home in defeat. Fewer than 100 soldiers returned with Coronado

Above: Huge herds of buffalo thundered over the Great Plains during the Age of Discovery. Below: The Grand Canyon of Arizona is one of North America's most spectacular sites, but Coronado's thirsty men were not impressed.

Chapter Five

After the Age of Discovery

The stories of the Age of Discovery all share a common theme: Europeans, in search of fortune, headed west across the Atlantic. Columbus, Cabot, and Magellan thought they would find their treasure by finding a water route to Asia. Conquistadors sought riches in the lands themselves. For the most part, the explorers did not find what they sought, but their discoveries redrew the map of the world.

The findings of early European explorers led to accurate world maps, such as this one from 1694.

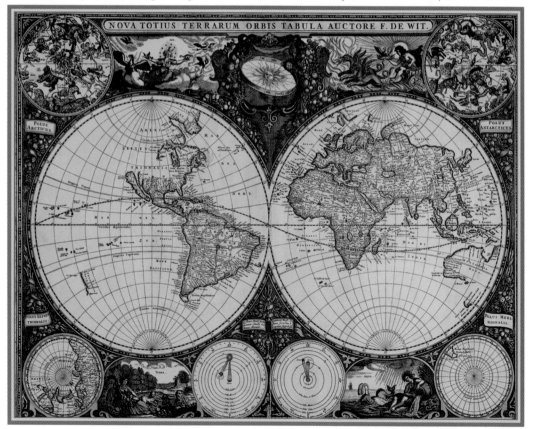

Columbus's landing on a beach in the Bahamas forever changed the lives of both Europeans and Indians. Some of the changes were small. For the first time, Europeans tasted foods of the New World—including corn, potatoes, pineapple, tobacco, and turkey. From Europe, they brought with them new crops, such as sugar cane and wheat, as well as horses, pigs, and other animals.

Though not on purpose, Europeans also brought devastating diseases like smallpox, malaria, and measles. Their bodies were used to these diseases and so had built up a resistance that protected them. To Indians, however, the diseases were brand-new—and therefore very powerful. Entire populations of Indians were wiped out.

Englishman William Penn (with hat and outstretched arms) made a peace treaty with Indians when he founded the colony of Pennsylvania in 1682. Penn's treaties with Indians were among the most successful in the New World.

Europeans introduced Indians to guns and Christianity. Many Indians were forced to take on this new religion. Often, they mixed their own religious traditions with those of the new one. In some places, European colonists forced Indians to work for them. In other places, they drove Indians out of the best land. Some white settlers formed alliances with the Indians and the two groups lived together, uneasily but peacefully.

"Everything that has happened since the ... discovery of the Americas has been so extraordinary that the whole story remains quite incredible to anyone who has not experienced it at first hand. ... It seems to ... silence all talk of other wonders of the world."

Bartolomé de Las Casas,
A Short Account of the
Destruction of the Indies, *1542*

In this 1890 illustration, an Indian chief informs fellow members of his tribe of the arrival of foreigners.

A white slave trader examines an African man, who will be sold like property. Slaves were brought to the Americas from Africa partly to replace Indian workers who had been wiped out by European diseases.

When Columbus sailed back to Spain in 1493, he left behind a group of sailors to form a colony in the new land. That colony did not survive. However, Columbus had opened the door for future settlements in the Americas. In turn, the colonies opened up the slave trade from Africa. Millions of Africans were kidnapped and brought to the Americas to work the land against their will.

"I say again that I stood looking at it, and I thought that no land like it would ever be discovered in the whole world."

Bernal Díaz del Castillo, The Conquest of New Spain, written around 1565

Columbus's arrival on the shores of the Americas was the result of a miscalculation. However, this mistake proved to be far more important than his original plan. Historians have called Columbus's landing in America the greatest event in world history. That morning on the beach in the Bahamas brought changes that continue to impact the world today.

Pilgrims arrived on the shores of present-day Massachusetts in 1620. The New World offered the early English settlers the opportunity to freely practice their religion.

Biographies

Vasco Núñez de Balboa (1475–1519)

A Spanish conquistador, Balboa explored the areas around present-day Panama. He crossed the Americas at their narrowest point, the Isthmus of Panama. In 1513, Balboa's search for gold led him to the Pacific Ocean, where he became the first European to see its eastern coast. Balboa's discovery proved to Europeans that North and South America were one landmass, not part of Asia.

John Cabot (ca.1450–ca.1499)

Giovanni Caboto was an Italian-born explorer who, in 1497, made the first British voyage to North America. Believing the land he reached was part of Asia, Cabot went in search of a short route to the riches of the Indies. He landed either on the eastern coast of Canada or the coast of Maine. Cabot's voyage gave Great Britain claims to North America, which led to the founding of British colonies there.

Christopher Columbus (1451–1506)

Columbus was the Italian explorer who, sailing for Spain, led the first European expedition across the Atlantic Ocean during the Age of Discovery. In 1492, Columbus left Spain in search of a water route to Asia. Instead, he landed in the Americas. This event has been called the greatest in the history of the world. It opened the door to the European colonization of North and South America.

Francisco Vásquez de Coronado (ca.1510–54)

Coronado was a Spanish conquistador who led a 7,000-mile (11,200 kilometers) expedition through the present-day American Southwest. From 1540 to 1542, Coronado searched in vain for legendary cities of gold. A group of his men became the first Europeans to see the Grand Canyon and the Great Plains.

Ferdinand Magellan (ca.1480–1521)

Magellan was a Portuguese explorer who led the first expedition to sail around the world. He and his men were also the first Europeans to cross the Pacific Ocean. Sailing for Spain, Magellan left in 1519 to find a sea route to Asia around the southern tip of South America. The passage he discovered was named the Strait of Magellan in his honor.

Giovanni da Verrazano (ca.1485–ca.1528)

Verrazano was an Italian explorer who sailed to North America under the French flag. He left in 1524 in search of the Northwest Passage. The Northwest Passage is a water route through or around North America. Verrazano did not find the passage, but he made important discoveries about the eastern coast of North America from North Carolina to Newfoundland, Canada.

Amerigo Vespucci (1454–1512)

Vespucci was an Italian explorer who was given credit for being the first to recognize that the Americas were not part of Asia. He was the first to use the term *New World*. The word *America* is the Latin version of his first name.

Timeline

50,000 BC
The first humans arrive in North America, by present-day Alaska.

AD 1000
Vikings reach the shores of what is now Canada.

1492
Columbus arrives in the Americas.

1497
John Cabot reaches the eastern shore of Canada or the coast of Maine.

1507
The Latinized version of Amerigo Vespucci's name—*America*—is used on a map to label the New World.

1509
The first Africans are kidnapped and brought to the Americas as slaves.

1513
Balboa becomes the first European to see the eastern shore of the Pacific Ocean.

1522
Members of Magellan's crew complete the first trip around the globe.

1524
France sends Giovanni da Verrazano to North America in search of a northern water route to Asia.

1540–42
Coronado leads an expedition through the American Southwest.

1585
Roanoke Island becomes the first British colony in North America.

1585

Glossary

Christianity (KRIHS-chee-AN-uh-tee)
a religion founded on the life and teachings of Jesus Christ; the main religion of Europe during the Age of Discovery

colony (KOL-uh-nee)
a group of people who settle in a distant land while remaining citizens of their original country; also the word for the place they settle

conquistador (kon-KEES-tuh-dohr)
a leader of the sixteenth-century Spanish expeditions that came to the Americas to find gold and convert Indians to Christianity

continent (KON-tuh-nuhnt)
one of seven main landmasses of Earth: Africa, Antarctica, Asia, Australia, Europe, North America, and South America

geography (gee-AH-gra-fee)
the study of the earth's features, such as bodies of water, mountains, and islands

Great Plains (GRAYT PLAYNZ)
a large grassland area in central North America that stretches from northern Canada into Texas and New Mexico

Indies (IHN-dees)
the word used during Columbus's day to refer to the areas now known as Iran, India, China, and Japan

legend (LEHJ-uhnd)
a story passed down from one generation to another that may not be true

mutiny (MYOO-tuh-nee)
rebellion against legal authority by refusing to obey orders and, often, attacking officers, especially aboard a ship

natives (NAY-tihvz)
people who originate, or come from, a certain place

navigation (NAV-uh-GAY-shuhn)
the science of guiding a ship from place to place

Vikings (VY-kihngz)
explorers who came from northern Europe between the eighth and eleventh centuries; Vikings traveled by sea to raid other lands

Further Resources

Web Links

Enchanted Learning—Zoom Explorers
www.enchantedlearning.com/explorers
This site is a handy reference for basic facts about explorers throughout time. Click on the letter of an explorer's last name to search for a short biography.

The Mariners' Museum—Age of Exploration
www.mariner.org/educationalad/ageofex/index.php
This site provides an overview of the history of exploration by sea. It also provides biographies of key explorers with links to maps of the routes they traveled.

PBS—Conquistadors
www.pbs.org/conquistadors
This site tells the story of the Spanish conquest in the Americas. It includes many illustrations, maps, timelines, and other study aids.

Books

Kramer, Sydelle. *Who Was Ferdinand Magellan?* Grosset & Dunlap, 2004.

Malam, John. *Columbus Reaches the Americas*. Smart Apple Media, 2003.

Stein, R. Conrad. *The Conquistadores: Building a Spanish Empire in the Americas*. Child's World, 2004.

Index